CLICK

A Modern day marketers GUIDE to getting the most out of SOCIAL MEDIA for your business

PLUS actionable tips to drive results on 3 top platforms – Facebook, Instagram and Youtube

Click

Click

Click

Introduction

Social Media has imploded onto the scene across the last decade and alongside that, has become an indispensable tool to businesses of all sizes.

With the opportunity for business owners to reach out, engage and learn from their potential customers like never before, it's become a vital and an expected form of marketing in todays world.

If you are not using social media as a marketing tool or if your current strategy could be improved, now is the time to make a change.

Marketing is a bridge between your business and the outside world and social media marketing especially gives you the power as a business owner to reach and niche in, on more

Click

of your target market than ever before. But, social media doesn't have to be wrapped up in jargon and difficult to learn theories. In fact, we find social media works best when we strip it back and keep it simple.

Across this book you are going to learn the social media tricks and tips that you can effectively implement into your business across the popular social media platforms to increase your reach to your target client and also increase their awareness of your business, brand and products. Success in social media marketing comes from building strong and long lasting relationships with followers that go beyond just 'chasing the sale.'

Creating and sharing the type of expertise and content that your followers will want to share

Click

with their friends, family and colleagues is the foundations for a strong social media campaign across the popular channels.

It allows you to attract and keep loyal followers and customers, connect with people inside of your niche and connect with potential customers for your business. Encouraging a community around your business through your social media and investing in creating relationships with those who interact with your brand and this openness and two-way conversation between customers and brands on social media is now something that billions of people now expect from the brands that they invest their time following and then go on to invest their money with.

We hope you find the following advice helpful, whether you are a complete social media

Click

novice and have been 'winging it' so far or whether you are a bit more savvy but are just looking for some extra ideas or tips to further drive your business forward.

General media hype, successful business stories in the media and the fact that everyone seems to be on some sort of social media, tell business owners today that building a strong presence on social media is essential. It's not to say a business couldn't do well without being on social media but they would be certainly missing opportunities to utilise networks and grow.

One of the biggest mistakes we see is business owners jumping in to a social media platform with no real clue of what they are doing or what they are going to do with it –with the vague hope that by showing up some of

Click

the time it will just work. Whilst, this may possibly work short term and there's a possibility you may get lucky, in most cases this will lead to poor results and a waste of your own time which is hugely demotivating, potentially discouraging you from social media marketing completely.

To ensure you are using social media for the best chance of success for your own business learn and then adopt the strategies inside of this book which will teach you how to encompass the power of social media marketing for business.

Before we begin it is important to learn some key practices and considerations for all of your social media marketing strategies. This will help you get a firm understanding of the kind of approach that works and also how to

Click

channel your efforts into a well planned, effective and logical direction.

Unless you have unlimited resources and a huge budget to go all in on every viable social media platform there is out there, the chances are you are better to focus your time and efforts into one or two social networks first. Narrowing down your choice to just a select few platforms will allow you to focus your efforts, grow your expertise on those channels and be the most time effective in your business too. It is important to acknowledge that although social media networks can be largely free – your time is not, and it is very valuable. There are thousands of social networks out there to choose from, but the good news is that you can start by narrowing it down by identifying where your target client

Click

and audience already 'hangs out.' The entire point of social media marketing is to put you in contact with, and in front of your best audience, so it's going to be a waste of resources to choose a platform where your target audience doesn't operate.

Unfortunately, there's no magic system where your future prospects will start to use the social platform of your choice just because you've created a profile. Instead, it's a much better idea to analyse which platforms your audience prefers and to seek them out on the networks they're already using. There are a few different ways you can discover where your ideal client is hanging out online but one of the most straightforward ways is to simply ask. Ask questions to target prospects about what social sites they like to use, which influencers they listen to, where they go to find new

Click

information online etc. You can also find out audience demographics from the social media sites themselves. Facebook for example, will identify the size of your target audience if you tell it about your target client. Alongside this researching the main social media channels will help you judge where best your content and brand voice will best be received. Joining Facebook, Twitter and Instagram are often the go-to choices for brands due to their sheer size and influence but there are more niche communities online too such as Pinterest where you may find you may make an impact more successfully. This is why it is important to define and assess your marketing goals and plan out the overall goals of your marketing strategy.

Click

If you don't currently set clear goals for your social strategy, don't worry you are definitely not alone! However, trying to navigate your social media and indeed deciding which platforms to be present on can be daunting and frustrating to achieve, without clear goals. Instead, you need to feel empowered to get down deep into your business marketing strategy and knowing everyday what you need to be doing in order to meet the needs of the clients you want to attract.

By defining clear goals you are able to refer to a pre made and measurable plan and hold yourself and your time accountable, after-all social media is an incredibly distracting place to be. Hopefully by now you are realising it's probably not ok to just 'wing it' and that setting

Click

actionable goals is a great start in building a solid social media marketing foundation.

Once you have set some broader objectives and smaller goals, you can then begin working on them to achieve specific targeted results throughout your social media marketing. More often than not, especially in the beginning, it is better to focus on engagement and building a presence. After a good amount of time, usually at least every month or so you can evaluate and measure those goals by using analytics and social media insight tools, we'll focus on this more in depth later in the book.

Your goals should give you an idea for your overall strategy and also help you decide on which content you want to share. To get an idea of the type of content that will resonate

Click

with your audiences you can carry out a short audit. Take some time to identify your audiences needs, interests on social media, identify what problems you and your business can help them overcome and what questions you can answer for them. Start to gather the type of content your audience prefers such as text, photo, info graphics, video and think about when they will be around to view it. You probably know the answer to some of these questions already; you can also use your competitors to help! First identify your competitors inside of your business niche, you probably know them already but a quick web search will tell you. Take a visit of their websites and social media profiles, make a note of how often they post blogs, and status updates and what content seems to perform best for them based on the numbers of

Click

comments, likes and shares. You can go further by looking at the tone of their posts, the topics used and how much of the content is original content and how much is shared posts from other feeds too. Use the type of information you gather as inspiration for you to mirror in your own social media copy, but also identify gaps and opportunities where you can do better.

One of the biggest tasks facing businesses on social media today is to consistently publish high quality content for their followers. A social media presence that appears abandoned is the digital equivalent of owning a shop and keeping the door locked. Consistency in posting boosts levels of engagement by enabling those who follow you to anticipate your next post and keeps followers coming back for more creating a stronger relationship

Click

with your audience. One of the best ways to help with this is to create a social media calendar. This will allow you to plan your activity or weeks or even months in advance. It allows you to build seasonal themes into your updates, stay ahead of trends and industry news and also prevents you from posting sub par content just because you need to publish something. In addition it can reduce stress. Many of us are busy and stressed with other areas of our life and business -- why make it worse by having to worry about what to post every single day? By planning posts for the entire week, or the entire month, you're able to reduce your everyday stress of figuring out what to post on that specific day, which is very time consuming and a productivity killer. Spontaneous posting to social media still has a place, but for the foundations of your overall

Click

strategy a content calendar is highly recommended. A simple way to plan a content strategy and prevent overwhelm is to create a daily theme across your socials for example – sharing a blog post on a Monday, doing a Live video on a Thursday etc. It is also worth noting that content can be repurposed. A piece of content such as a blog can sometimes be repurposed and marketed as four or five different content pieces for social media: tweet, make a video, share some of it to Facebook, turn it into an Infographic for Pinterest etc. In addition to saving you time and resources, repurposing content also drives traffic and creates engagement across your other marketing channels.

Click

1. Providing Value Up Front

The vast majority of social media users do not visit Facebook, Twitter, and Instagram to be given the hard sell by businesses online. They use them to engage and interact with families and friends, to be entertained, informed and kept up to speed with news and current affairs.

It is your job as social media marketers to convince people to enjoy having your business as something that is part of their everyday lives and a brand that they enjoy interacting with. You do this by building trusting and loyal relationships, by being friendly, sharing great content and having a genuine interest in the people who follow your brand. You should also seek to actively help your followers on social media, including the odd promotional post in between, which as long as the rest of your

Click

strategy is on target, your audience should be more receptive to.

Change your mindset with your social media strategy from "what can I sell you?" to "What can I do to help you?'

In order to win the approval and acceptance of customers in the future, businesses are finding it more important than ever to provide value first before asking for anything in return. With competition from other businesses organic (non paid) reach (the number of people who see your content) is at an all-time low, it is important to include content in your marketing strategy that connects with people on an emotional and personal level to ensure you stand out in a busy space.

Just like in the real world, people flock to the brands that they love and trust rather than the

Click

ones with overly *sale-sy* messages who are only interested in selling them something.

You should think about the headings below, (which we break down into the word VIRAL) when deciding whether your following will consider your content valuable to them.

Value

Is this piece of content valuable to your follower? Is it providing something to your end user? This does not need to be a specific freebie or item but value also comes in the form of entertainment, explainers, education and much more. Content that is considered valuable enhances your follower experience with your brand.

Inspirational

Click

Is your content inspirational? Is it creating a good feeling about your overall business, product or service?

Relevant

Is your content relevant? Is the content you are sharing on trend, relevant to the industry you work in or to current affairs? Is the content relevant to the platform you are posting it on?

Authentic

Is the content you are sharing authentic? Does it fit in with your overall brand and tone? Does it align with your business message and values?

Looks Good

Does this piece of content look good? Is it going to make followers stop on their feeds

Click

and take notice? Is it formatted for the platform you are sharing it on?

The content that you share to your audience should hit these points. Every now and then it is good practice to go back over your last few posts on social media and just check that you are still providing value and serving a purpose by posting to your social media. All of this great content will build a positive image around your brand and slowly convert into sales.

BE PATIENT IT TAKES TIME

Social media success does not happen overnight, just like in real life friendships and relationships take time to build. Some people

Click

are going to take longer to warm to you and convert into paying customers than others. Think about it – how long did it take you to befriend your newest friend? And I don't mean the person you casually hang out with or work with, I'm talking about the person you trust and share your secrets with...It probably took some time, right? Maybe even a lot of time! Maybe, you didn't even like each other at first, but once you began talking, there was a common connection. You shared interests and life stories, and before you knew it – you'd found someone you connected with. Now imagine if all of that took place online – in an environment where you couldn't read their facial expressions or was only able to get to know their humour through words and emojis. That would have probably taken longer, right? This is exactly how relationship building is on

Click

social media and it is something as business owners we have to work towards everyday. Converting social media followers into raving fans of your brand and then sales is a long game and if you are not serious about working at it consistently than unfortunately you are already setting yourself up for failure.

Our job as marketers on social media is to locate people who are a good fit to connect with our product or service. Maybe they have the same interests as you or you share mutual connections or maybe you have a bit of both but once we identify the people we need to connect with we begin down a road towards developing that relationship, we answer questions they have, we provide them with value, we show up consistently and create credibility in our business, we value them as a

Click

member of our community and converse with them.

All of this takes time. We can't be pushy, we can't get on the soapbox, and we must be thoughtful and respectful because that's how relationships are built. It is best to keep this in mind from the beginning. There is no super fast recipe that will 'get followers fast' other than scams which you want to stay clear of. It may be tempting to use services such as this across the web to rack up numbers, this is just a vanity metric and you'll only end up with hundreds of random strangers – and bot accounts – who don't care about you nor your business. It is much better to have 50 loyal, engaged and interested followers than 5000 that are not.

If you remember nothing else from this section remember that friendships, whether in real life,

Click

or as a part of a social media marketing campaign don't just happen by throwing yourself out there and shouting about what you do for others to find. They require careful consideration, introductions and a gradual building of trust so that our clients to get to know us like us and trust us so that in turn they are then more likely to buy with us.

SHOW UP, DON'T GIVE UP

Having a valued presence on social media means showing up and engaging with your followers. You cannot create meaningful relationships with people by showing up, posting for a few weeks and then giving up! Most social media runs off an algorithm that works by bringing users the content they are,

Click

and could be interested in and so if you think that by taking an ad-hoc approach and posting as and when they will reward your account you can think again!

Facebook, Instagram, and Twitter for example base user's timelines by prioritising accounts they engage with and the content that will most likely resonate with that user. For example products that have been searched for on the Internet then pop up as ads over on social feeds. Interest and engagement leads to clicks and then leads to sales. The less you post on the more social sites like Instagram and Facebook the less of your content will show up on timelines. The more social you are (providing you are not just spamming) the more prominence you get on news feeds. For most social media networks posting one to two times a day is a good start, but as a minimum

Click

you should be aiming to show up with engaging and high quality posts at least a couple of times a week, this enables your posts to be seen in the news feeds of your engaged followers.

In addition to regular posting to ensure that the content you put out into the world is seen by as many people as possibly it must be top quality – this is what we call *value-add (or just value)* posts and something that you share that your users find inspirational, entertaining, relevant or helpful (as broken down above VIRAL) so that they comment, like, share, visit your profile or click.

The more a user engages with your brand on social media the more they are likely to continue to do so in the future as that content becomes favoured above others on their newsfeeds. Facebook's complex algorithm,

Click

factors in over one thousand different considerations to determine what appears on its end users newsfeeds. Not only are you competing with other businesses in your industry for attention, you are also competing for space over interactions with their friends and family, from groups they are members of and the paid for ads too. If a fan of your page never *sees* any posts from you because you are inactive or they ignore your posts for a prolonged period of time because they aren't relevant to them and they aren't engaging with your content enough your posts may disappear from that persons feed altogether.

To ensure that your posts aren't ignored and are effective in reaching your fans you are going to need to create and share posts that encourage engagement.

Click

WHAT IS ENGAGEMENT

Social media engagement counts anytime a user interacts with your account and we have discovered why it is important for users to be interacting in ways such as follows, likes, re-tweets, shares with your account. Increasing social media engagement starts with a plan. You may be thinking 'Do you really need a plan for responding to people on the Internet?' and the answer is YES.

A solid plan for your social media engagement and strategy helps ensure every engagement you have on social media is not only useful to the person you're talking to, but also beneficial to your business as well.

Click

Businesses usually approach their social media strategies in one of two ways: what we call, the soapbox method vs. the dinner party method.

The *soapbox* method – Too many businesses on social media use the platforms they use as a soapbox. The place where they can shout out about their business and yell about their product to the masses where they remain pretty much out of reach themselves. There is nothing social about this method and there are few quicker ways to alienate people on social media than by constantly telling them how great you are. Perhaps it is more relatable to imagine you were at a networking event or dinner party and there's one person there who talks about nothing other than themselves, *how amazing they are, the holidays they have*

Click

booked and have been on, the amazing business deal they have just landed etc.

We all know someone like this guest—people who talk without listening, who seem to think that what they have to say is as fascinating to everyone else as it is to them, and who don't seem to understand that listening is an important part of communicating and connecting to others.

Well, just like that dinner guest turned you off into getting to know them, followers today are also turning off to businesses who use this marketing method.

The *dinner party* method – The businesses using the method above may be getting marketing messages out into the world about their business and products but they are leaving little or no room for others to chip in

Click

with valuable conversations and insights around the conversation.

Here's a breakdown into how to take a more *dinner party* approach to your social media marketing.

You're a polite host, and you're setting a beautiful table: You have started an account on a social media channel, you've added your branding, some copy and your website, and you're starting to post interesting and relevant content.

You're inviting a mix of interesting people who are relevant to you interesting to each other: You're following your peers, industry leaders, media, and other people who you know will be interested in what you're offering.

You're creating interesting conversation around the table, and these interesting people are participating in the conversation with you

Click

and with each other: You are liking and sharing content from the people you're following, as well as participating in conversations with your community and your followers, *and* these folks are talking back to you.

Everyone has a wonderful time and comes back for your next dinner party, bringing some new interesting friends with them: New followers are finding you and engaging with you by liking your content and sharing it with their friends.

Once you do start to use your own social media platforms as a way to engage and converse with people, you'll be able to leverage it in a more meaningful way including increasing leads, increasing your brand awareness and offering better customer support.

Click

The stronger someone connects to your business and brand on social media the more likely it is that they will remember you and pass on your referral to their friends and family.

Click

2: The types of Posts to Post on Social Media

We have covered the foundations of social media marketing and it's now time to look at the kinds of content and posting strategies that will help your marketing strategy strive.

Regardless of what your business is and what platform(s) you choose to work with, the overall goal of any social media activity is to move customers closer to purchasing your product or hiring your service and so it is essential as business owners to know what kind of content our audience responds to in order to entice them into making the sale. In this chapter we will look at strategies to adopt in your business marketing but also tips to make you a better content creator in order to

Click

inspire your audience to take action on that content.

First and foremost to be able to provide relevant and inspiring content to your followers you are going to need to do your research. The more relevant your posts are, the more success you will have. Taking the time to really know your audience will see a return tenfold in your interactions and engagements on your posts on social media. Too often we see businesses that create campaigns first and then try and find their audience, and hope they respond to it when in reality it needs to be the other way around.

You should always have your audience at the forefront of your mind when posting on social media.

It most definitely isn't about you!

Click

Identifying your target customer goes beyond just thinking about their demographics i.e.- facts that determine who the customer is such as their age, income, gender, occupation level but also their psychographics. Psychographics identify the *reasons* your customers and the information to both your audience demographics and psychographics can be found by using social media insights, online research, surveys and also personal interviews and chatting with past clients and future prospects. Ask your target market about things that aren't directly relevant to selling your product or service. Ask the kind of "get to know you" questions you would ask in a real life introduction. Choose topics that are interesting for your market research, but also ask the questions because you just want to

Click

know your audience better. Companies that use social media to show they understand and care about the audience they serve are the ones that get attention, get followers, and get shared and referrals because they're trying to make a genuine connection rather than just sell.

Once you have identified your target customer and their interests, needs, obstacles and challenges they have you can develop content and social media posts that provides solutions to those issues and speaks to their interests. Taking your findings further you can also learn what language your ideal clients use to communicate, and then you can replicate this in your posts to ensure your content resonates with your ideal clients. This helps to show your followers that you truly understand them but

Click

also helps you build solid common ground to start that relationship between them as a follower and you, your brand. Also, if you use language and tone like your followers would use in everyday language, your message is more likely to be heard, remembered and repeated.

Although infusing your social media posts with the language of your target audience is a good strategy to deepen connections, your overall social message should be written in your own voice. Your voice (or your brand voice) refers to the personality and emotion across all of your marketing activities and social interactions. Your brand voice is primarily your or your company's personality. This voice needs to be consistent throughout the content you create and the posts you share on social platforms, as well as any engagement you

Click

have on those networks. This consistency will help your audience connect with you emotionally, as well as build trust, and make your social posts instantly recognisable.

You can bond with your audience over the content you put out online by ensuring that everything you write is created with their wants and needs in mind.

Keep professional and handle complaints well It is incredibly important to stay professional and positive across your channels. You are going to want your audience to feel connected to and inspired by your posts. In some of your posts, you may choose to share your opinion or take a stand on something important to you and your brand. But there's a difference between taking a stand and attacking or criticizing others. Whatever you do, avoid criticizing anyone (or any business) publicly.

Click

Unlike in the past, social media gives your business instant and effective exposure to customers 24 hours a day, 7 days a week. Customers also get that access to *you* and this has led to a revolution in customer service and also customer expectation. With the instantaneousness of social media people's expectations for swift and effective responses to their queries and problems is higher than ever. There's a lot of advice online regarding acceptable reply times on social media, with many having an optimal reply time of around 40 minutes. For the vast majority of businesses this isn't going to be a realistic target it is still important that you deal with customer service issues as soon as possible, 24 hours (on weekends too, if you can manage it) is acceptable to most people. Use the about section and consider setting up an

Click

out of hours message responder on your profiles to arm customers with the methods to contact you and also to set expectations for how long they can expect to wait for a reply. Deal with customer complaints and service issues professionally and in a courteous manner and within a time frame that the resources within your business allow. You cannot change what has happened to upset your customer, but you do have the power to affect the next part of the conversation.

Adopt the BEET strategy – *Be Empathetic Every Time.* We are all human and customers realise this and will respect you a lot more if you apologise and empathise with their viewpoint, even if you don't agree. Customer service on social media is a spectator sport, when you are addressing customers on any of

Click

your platforms you are really addressing more than just that one person and you should treat your replies as if you are talking to a group of people, current customers and future potential ones. When handling complaints and queries you are satisfying the original customer but you are also re-establishing your businesses values. It should take no more than 2 replies to establish this. Any complaints after this should be done in a more private setting and away from a public setting

.

Ask questions and create discussions
We have already established the importance of getting to know your audience. Asking questions and creating key discussions around interests relating to your product and service and those of your audience allows your followers to get to know you too. These

can be about a product or event related to your business or field, a quick getting to know you and your business quiz or just about current affairs. Questions or polls that ask for preferences such as *option a* over *option b,* ones that ask for opinions and even just ending a caption or status with *'do you agree?'* or *'what do you think?'* is enough to encourage your audience to get involved with your brand. The simplest of questions can attract some pretty impressive levels of engagement (and audience insight) particularly if it takes the user little or no effort to respond. Similarly *'fill in the blank'* kind posts are successful because fans are able to communicate quickly and with minimal effort for example: *'If you could live anywhere in the world, it would be _____'*

Click

Story Selling

Everybody has a story to tell. Stories have been used from the dawn of time to pass down valuable information and engage people's attention. Stories are incredibly humanistic and appeal to the emotional parts of our brains. Creating an emotional connection between your brand and audience puts you in an enviable position above your competitors. Social media is an incredible outlay for connecting with your target market and allowing them to get to know you and the story you are wishing to involve them in. In the past, reaching the masses via advertising was expensive and only possible through large media firms, now social media allows you to tell your story at scale and build powerful relationships with your customers.

Click

Stories about real people are relatable and meaningful, use social media as a platform for consumers to really get to know your business and create a stronger connection than just by viewing products or the services that you sell. Talk about the people behind your brand, every business has a story and a founder, take some time to plan how best you can share your story and how it can be told in such a way that it creates an emotional connection. The more real a brand story is, the more likely it is to resonate with others and create trust. As important as it is to share stories around the creation of your company along with the passion for what you do, it is similarly important to use social media to portray stories relating to your brand values. Building confidence in your brand is imperative to encourage clients to try you, and to gain their

Click

loyalty over a rival brand, product or company. Sharing stories relating around how your company upholds its promises are powerful trust builders.

Share stories as to how your product or service improves the lives of the people who use it. Incorporate it into a story around people you want to help, why do you care about them? How do you want to help them? People are drawn to content that educates, entertains, inspires and even celebrates them.

Much like the reasons behind why you started your story, people want to also know how you do what you do. Incorporating the 'how to' of your products production or process into your brands social presence can be especially impactful. For example if you use unique technology or sustainably sourced materials sharing the processes behind your business

Click

educates and provide transparency and insight into how you run your business which creates trust.

In sharing your story it is important to create a narrative and take your readers or viewers on a journey.

Some ways to do that are:

Problem/solution

Before/after

Tutorials

Personal stories

Customer Testimonials

Whilst sharing your own stories is important, sharing those from your customer will be more effective in attracting new audiences to your brand. Your past

Click

customers and clients will have fun and interesting stories about how you and your product or service fit into and enhanced their life. Often this will be more interesting content than you can come up with yourself and can offer new ideas or perspective to market your product. Encourage your customers to share their content and tales with you, through text testimonials, videos of them using your product and photos. Come up with a unique and memorable hashtag for your business to allow users to easily share and for you to easily find them and feature them as part of your content strategy. Doing so will excite those you mention and further develop their loyalty to your brand, encouraging them to spread even more love about the product or service you provided. This also helps to

Click

build a strong community around your product and act as social proof as to how your brand positively impacts on others.

Solve problems and create authority
An effective way to influence social media users into connecting with you is to position yourself and your brand as an authority in your market. A source that they like and respect and come to, to receive information. Brand authority is mainly described as the high recognition of a brand's ability and expertise within its sector. "Authority" is something that everyone in content marketing wants, however it's not something that everyone knows how to get and keep it. Google priorities content with authority higher than those without and so it's a great SEO tool

Click

alongside the status it will bring your brand amongst customers and competitors alike. Brand authority is built through consistency, patience and a well thought out strategy. One of the most effective ways to build brand authority and expertise online is through written and video content and making it visible to your audience. Having a blog or video channel within your niche is a great asset. A blog will allow you to position yourself as an expert in your field and show your customers that you are knowledgeable and also that you are interested in helping your consumers.

Gaining recognition comes hand and hand with brand authority. The more recognition your brand gets, the more people will see your company as a force to be reckoned with. Testimonials and reviews from

Click

previous clients build brand authority, reply to mentions you get across social media. You also need to show your authority and have confidence in yourself and your services and products. Be sure to add any certificates, awards and qualifications that you have that are relevant. When you are confident in your ability and in your brand, so are your customers.

Images are not just for Instagram. Social media feeds are noisy places, catching and keeping your audience's attention is becoming increasingly more difficult. Visuals should be an essential and core part of your social media strategy. According to Twitter, Tweets with photos receive an average of 35% more Retweets

Click

and on Facebook, posts that included photographs were found to have a 37% increase in engagement. Social media images are so in demand that Google has reported a year on year rise in the search term 'social media image' since 2009.

Don't get caught up in the trap of creating stand out, flashy visuals for your social media for the sake of it or to the detriment of your overall marketing message. It's typically best to keep your images crisp and simple, whilst certain instances may call for busier types of photographs you want to pull your audience in with a clear message that leaves no room for confusion. Steer clear of the types of images that need explanation or a caption to make sense of what you are trying to convey. Visuals with human connections perform well, much like

Click

telling a story followers connect to human emotions.

In order for your followers to recognise your visual content as soon as it appears in their newsfeed you should brand your images - this can be achieved adding a logo, website or URL to the image. You should choose a consistent colour palette, photo filter and fonts to reflect your brand personality. The colours, filters and fonts used in your images will strongly affect how your users perceive your brand, consider each brand element with care and think about the kinds of feelings your brand imagery will convey, e.g. – cheery, nostalgic, serious, romantic etc. You may consider using a template for the content you create, there are plenty of free apps and design software that will help you with this and having a template will not

Click

only save time but it will also help create a strong brand presence and familiarity over time with your social media.

In order to decide what kind of templates and images to use across your platforms study the performance of your past posts and take note of the ones that trigger responses from your audience and the ones that do not. When you figure out what works, simply replicate and give more of this to your audiences.

Physically creating the amount of visuals you need is beyond most small businesses budgets and time constraints. Luckily, there are lots of online tools to find and edit graphics that can be shared online. Natural stock photographs perform best so consider this when choosing the images you'll use in your business. Whether you have used a

Click

free or paid for image – always read and understand the terms of use - whether accreditation is required or not and whether the image is able to be used for commercial purposes.

The jargon can be confusing on stock image websites, so it's worth learning the lingo to avoid at best embarrassing complaints on your socials, at worst a complex legal situation.

The three categories to become familiar with are Public Domain (PD), Royalty Free (RF) and Right Managed (RM).

Stock photographs that are in the public domain are free to use without a license. If you are not big on legal jargon and would rather not mess around with licenses or pay for use, then the public domain is the way

Click

to go. Some photographs in the public domain require no attribution but do make sure you read the details of the image before sharing.

A royalty free license is the most common type of license when it comes to stock photography. It typically allows for a one-time payment that will then allow you, the advertiser, to use the photograph across several mediums without the need to buy the license again.

Right-managed licenses allow single use of the stock image as specified by the license. This may not be the most convenient way and can prove costly if you use these images often, however you can pay for exclusive rights of the stock image to avoid other rival companies using the same imagery and clients becoming confused in

Click

the future. It's important to note that right managed licenses cover only a single use of the image, and so if you wanted to run a different kind of advert or upload it to another channel you will have to purchase another kind of license to allow you to do that.

Some great sites for free stock images are:

http://www.unsplash.com
http://www.pexel.com
http://www.pixabay.com

Remember, with any image that is not yours to always read and understand the terms of use.

Click

Show customers using your products or services

Sharing images of real customers and past clients using and enjoying your product creates a vast amount of social proof. Using images in this way are powerful in converting followers into buyers because it helps viewers associate positive emotions with your brand. Pictures showcasing other people are proven to get higher engagement too. Everyone with a smartphone is now a content creator and this makes it extremely easy to share experiences with your brand as they happen via social media. Encourage your customers to do that whether they are at your premises, out and about or at home. You can create "selfie spots" and have

Click

purpose made signs in your premises, ask followers to share a picture of themselves in the comments of them using your product or run a competition over on Instagram with a branded hashtag. Get into the habit of actively encouraging your customers to tag or mention your profile in updates using your photographs, the relevant social media will notify you of the tag and then you can save these pictures for use in future content. Give credit of course but by then mentioning the original user you are making them feel special deepening that customers connection to your brand. Tagging will also mean their friends and followers are more likely to see the content too, further increasing your reach. Group this 'user-generated' type of content in your phone or as a saved board on Pinterest or saved

Click

album on Facebook or Instagram so that they are easy for you to find when planning future posts.

User generated content works amazingly well even in the digital era because word of mouth referrals are still an influential marketing tool. Including a way for followers and fans to share their own content with your brand and have you share it back will set you apart from others in your field. User generated content also brings a sense of community around your brand, which we explored earlier in the book. Instead of there being a gap between marketer (that's you) and consumer (them) and brands constantly trying to win consumers over, user generated content brings everyone together and celebrates

Click

them. Another benefit to this kind of content is that it's free. Whether users are sharing stories, testimonials, pictures or videos with your brand they are doing it totally unpaid, to either share an experience and build a connection with like-minded people or to be in with a chance of winning something. This obviously has benefits over forking out hundreds or thousands on marketing campaigns. The beauty of user-generated content is that your clients and customers run the show, and you don't have to empty your pockets on campaigns that may not perform well.

Share Inspirational Images and Quotes

A type of image post that performs well on social media is inspirational and

Click

motivational quotes. There are entire social media accounts and websites dedicated to just quotes. In addition to their ability to stir an immediate emotional response they are highly shareable.

Since social media is about being sociable it is your job as the marketer in your business to give your fans content that is inspirational, positive, entertaining, humorous or informative. Negativity should be left for other accounts; people desire content that makes them feel better. One of your goals should be to connect with your audience to increase trust. Quotes are used a lot by even the biggest brands on social media when producing non-promotional posts.

Click

Social media contains an epic amount of content for your audience to consume. Who has the time or attention span? Whilst longer form content can help with SEO, it can also overwhelm, your audience may prefer and appreciate your content more in bite-sized chunks of micro content. Social posts that link to articles suggest that there's more reading and work involved for the follower, and as a result some people may be less likely to click through. Quotes on the other hand are quick and easily consumed pieces of micro-content. Some of the time your followers will want to know the whole story often the highlights are enough. Whereas blogs and videos are like reading a whole book, quotes emphasize the most critical points in short form. Quotes require little commitment from the person

Click

consuming them. Used strategically and practically inside of your overall social media strategy quotes will increase your awareness and visibility whilst still expressing your all important brand message.

Quotes also have the ability to make your readers feel something. When the content you share is both visually and emotionally appealing you'll see an increase in engagement across your socials, which over time will form connections with your audience. When you make people feel happy, inspired or laugh they associate you with positive emotion.

Using the quotes of others and using this as part of an influencer strategy can get you recognition inside of the industry and also exposure to their audiences too. Find quotes

Click

that would resonate with your audience and align with your brand from influencers or industry leaders and add them to your blogs or share them on social media.

Quotes are not just about motivating others; there are a few different ways in which you can incorporate quotes into your social media strategy. You can share quotes about trends in your industry, statistics, ones that evoke humour, quotes from blog snippets – either your own or others, you can use customer testimonials as blogs too. Another reason why quotes make for a great kind of image to use in your overall social media strategy is that they are easily branded. It doesn't matter what the quote is about you can easily pop it into a program such as Canva and make it on brand for your audience.

Click

Quotes are also educational. Audiences also come to social media to learn and to discover information relating to topics that peak their interest. Quotes are one way to convey information and educate other whilst increasing visibility and awareness. With quotes being a form of micro-content you may be wondering how you get enough information in them to educate. On platforms such as Facebook and Instagram, share a thought-provoking quote as a visual and then explain more about the quote in the caption. On Twitter, your posts need to be brief. You are able to use up to four images to convey your message and you can use this to convey your point rather than trying to cram it into a few different tweets. Developing a strategy including informative quotes is worth doing. Over

Click

time, the accumulation of your content forms an opinon of your brand that will be helpful and knowledgeable, turning followers into fans and purchasers.

Showcase behind the scenes

Behind-the-scenes content involves showing your followers what's happening behind the brand that they love. It involves things like company culture and the everyday workings and goings on of your business. Summed up it's showing the process and not just the product. Showcasing behind the scenes gives your brand the chance to connect with the community you are building on a personal level, making your business relatable and more approachable.

Click

Use your camera phone to snap photos of the behind-the-scenes workings of your business, the coffee meeting you are having, the project you are working on, where you work from, treats you have bought to celebrate the end of the working week, welcoming a new member of staff whatever it is document it and share it with you audiences. It's an effective way to build quick and lasting rapport with consumers of your content and also a way to showcase transparency helping your audience to trust you.

Showcasing the processes and efforts involved in your business success makes your followers appreciate and value what you do more. By sharing your values and what matters to you as an individual and in your business you attract other people with

Click

similar principles and involving your community in the general day to day processes and stories in your business and even giving them a say over some of the decisions you make gives your followers a sense of belonging creating deeper loyalties to your brand.

Memes and Gifs

Memes (usually humoured captioned images grouped into categories) are hugely shareable on social media. Animated Gifs are an easy way for brands to add a fun element to content. Check out Giphy or MemeGenerator for examples to use within your own social media. Humorous and cute images do well on all social media

Click

platforms. Memes and Gifs play off content that is created by other people so you don't need to create an original video yourself, saving you time. They also help create a sense of belonging or community because your audience all share in the same reference or enjoy the same joke. If you can make your audience laugh, you'll attract followers and help those people relate to you.

By definition, memes and gifs are supposed to be shared, and so the content that you produce or use is often reposted and shared across the Internet for an even wider reach.

This type of content is often on trend or related to a particular event. For example The Superbowl halftime show or a particular popular Netflix show. Sharing

Click

content that is on trend makes your brand more real, modern and human, whilst sharing content that relates to current topic affairs or popular culture makes your brand appear authentic and fresh.

Whilst memes and gifs are appealing to audiences it can be difficult to incorporate them as a business whilst maintaining your brand consistency. However as this kind of content is becoming more mainstream, even high end lifestyle brands have begun experimenting with them to stay relevant and grow followings. Memes can expand your reach significantly especially if your ideal client is a millennial or younger. The key is to be authentic and not overly conservative when sharing this kind of content. Edgy content can demonstrate that your brand has a personality and a unique

Click

voice, which can set your brand apart from other competitors. When your social media content delights and entertains those who follow and interact with it, your content is more likely to be shared, reaching a wider audience, which in turn makes it easier to generate sales and leads.

You can incorporate memes and gifs easily into your wider social media strategy without watering down your brand message. You can share something related to a national holiday or react to popular culture such as a show your ideal client is likely to watch, the tip is to not share too many and to always be aware of your brands voice.

Click

4. Using Facebook For Your Business

Your target audience is almost guaranteed to be using Facebook. With over a billion active users it's the most visited social media network in the world. Across this chapter you'll learns tips and strategies to build a following and market your business on Facebook as well as ensuring those followers are highly engaged in your business.

Before we dive in, it pays to build solid foundations in order to get your brand presence on this network set up and seen correctly so that you can be found and have maximum impact when your fans do find you.

Set up a Page, not a profile

When you sign up to Facebook, you are assigned a personal profile by default. These are designed for non-commercial use. For you and your business to be able to take advantage of the marketing features Facebook has designed for businesses, you must create a separate Facebook page.

Although there are businesses that operate without a page and use a profile, it's only going to be a matter of time before Facebook clamp down on this and deletes the account. If you are using a personal page for your business, stop doing it! Firstly it doesn't project professionalism, it's also connected to all of your own personal information and will send customers a message when it's your birthday for example, and your business will even have

Click

a gender! It's not giving off the best vibes or brand message about your business and potentially harming it too.

By having a page you are able to access insights about your customers which you are not able to do with just a profile, even if you are not thinking about insights now, it's helpful that Facebook is just busy collecting that information for when you would like to use it in the future. Insights will tell you everything from your audience profile to what time they are on Facebook, the best times to post and what posts your audience has responded to most - all helpful stuff to help you share content in a more targeted way. With a personal profile you are only able to write posts to connect with your audience who will be 'friends' and not 'fans' If you have a business page you are able to

Click

utilise several tabs allowing you to add video, product pages, an online shop and even a newsletter sign up. You also aren't able to run competitions or contests from a personal profile, well – you can but you'll be breaching Facebook terms and conditions and could have your profile removed. Another reason to ditch that Facebook profile and set up a page is that you are limited to only 5000 friends, which seriously limits your business potential for growth. You may be thinking that you'd be laughing all the way to the bank with 5000 customers however that would require 100% conversion of every single one of your friends to a sale, which, is impossible. Having a business page gives you access to post scheduling which can make your life as a business owner much easier as you can plan

Click

ahead and not have to worry about forgetting to post to your business profile. You want to be actively putting your business in front of your target customer at the times you are most relevant to them. For example have you ever noticed those takeaway ads pop up on your device on a Saturday night during The X Factor? To stick with the food analogy, offering a promotion on food, just when everyone starts to get hungry will probably influence customers into clicking an offer more than the same post after dinner time, when they are full and overcoming their post-dinner slump! If you are a business that has customers in other time zones, scheduling will save you from having to get up at 3am to put out a post that makes sense to your customers at that time. Personal profiles do not offer a scheduling tool.

Click

Having a business page rather than running from your personal profile allows you to activate places. This is a useful tool that allows your customers to 'check in' and let their friends know that they are at your store, work premises or restaurant and a great way to allow your customers to naturally promote your business.

Setting it up right, the first time

Chances are when you chose to start a business you set up a Facebook page with little thought to the set up of your business page. Try to keep your business name short and easy to remember, it is good practice to simply use your business name. If your business does go on to create Facebook ads

Click

having a short Facebook page name will work in your favour as the headline space on Facebook ads is limited and you only have 25 characters to play with. Think about choosing something that is easily to spell, if there are multiple different ways to spell something in your business name choose the most common spelling. You don't want to direct someone to a competitor because they cannot find you on Facebook.

Set up a URL for your Facebook page and ideally name it after your business. This makes it much easier for people to find you on Facebook and is the web address that leads people to your business page. Think carefully about your URL, as you are only able to change this once before Facebook locks this down.

Click

Fill in as much of your business detail as possible in the 'about' section for your Facebook Page including your business address, contact details, website information and other social media handles. Putting the effort into these sections makes your Facebook page helpful to customers finding it. Putting a search engine keyword rich about section will help your page be found by popular search engines. The about section is one of the first places people will look when they come to your page so keep this in mind and write up some of your best copy. Consider using headings that best aligns with your brand -- a general description, a mission, company information, or your story -- with brief, yet descriptive copy. By doing so, your audience can get a sense of what your page is about clearly before deciding whether to like it.

Click

Choose an effective and optimised cover and page picture.

Your Facebook page cover photograph can be viewed to anyone who finds your page, so make sure you are using the advertising space to it's fullest potential. The ideal cover photo size is 851 x 315 pixels. If the image is any smaller, Facebook will stretch the image, which can leave it appearing blurry. You are able to use a carousel of images to tell a brand story and set a video as your Facebook Page cover. Consider what is best for your brand. An effective cover photo would be a powerful image that conveys what you do and communicates who you are, a collage or

Click

carousel of images of your best products, an image highlighting a current offer or a customer testimonial. You can periodically change your cover and profile photo as often as you like. If you're going to use text in your cover photo, keep that text concise. Your photo will be much more informative and engaging without it in, less than 20% of text is a good ratio to work with. Since your profile picture is viewed on the left, you want to add some balance to your Facebook cover photo design by having the focus of the image on the right. This also allows for your cover photograph to be more mobile friendly. Do make sure that your cover photograph is perfectly aligned and mobile optimised. Whereas your cover photo displays at 820 pixels wide by 312 pixels tall on a desktop, it displays only the center 640 pixels wide by

Click

360 pixels tall on smartphones. Be wary when creating your cover image for your business that it works for both. You can add a description to cover photograph images and it's good practice to use this to include a link either to your website or a relevant product for example. The description will also appear when someone hovers a mouse cursor over the image, another reason to include one. Whilst your cover photo dominates your Facebook page, your profile picture is seen all over the site, in the news feed of all of your followers, in all comments and replies and it also overlays your cover photo. The recommended size for your profile picture is 180 x 180 pixels, but it is displayed at 160 x 160 on your Facebook business profile and as small as 48 x 48 pixels in comments on the news feed. You should choose an image

Click

synonymous with your brand and one recognisable even in its smallest form. Upload a large square image, when uploaded Facebook will automatically scale it down, when clicked on it will still look sharp. As with the cover image upload a description and add a link to the profile photo. Ensure that your profile and cover image compliment each other and are on brand.

Make use of the call to action button. In 2014, Facebook rolled out clickable call to action buttons that are designed to bring your businesses most important objective to the forefront of your Facebook profile. Experiment with different call to action buttons and see how your audience responds. Facebook will show you how many people click on your call-to-action button under the weekly metrics on the right side of your Facebook Page so you

Click

are able to track what works best for your business.

To be able to promote your Facebook Page on your website embed a like button in a suitable spot on your website. When you set up the plugin, if you are able to check the options to 'show friends' and 'show page posts' as this will ensure that it shows viewers the profile photo of any of their friends who already like your page. You can include a like and share plugin button underneath blog posts and products on your website too to encourage visitors to share their love of your brand on their own social media accounts.

A Facebook Crash Course in Marketing

Click

Now that your Facebook page is set up correctly, it's looking great and you are encouraging people to visit it, it's time to delve deeper and explore the ways in which you can use Facebook as an advertising platform to promote your business. Throughout this chapter we'll be exploring hints and tips to use in conjunction with the overall strategies described in previous chapters.

Setting up your Personal Profile for Business

As we have already explained in the previous chapter, using your personal profile specifically for business purposes is against Facebook rules and hopefully by now you have got the memo that it's also not going to be great for

Click

your image or business to do that. However, there are a number of little strategies that you can apply on your personal profile that can help support your business promotion.

List your place of work

If a customer searches for your business and comes across your personal profile you'll want to make it easy to direct that person on to your business page. Head to the 'Intro' section at the top of your profile and in the 'Work' section add your job title and then search for your Facebook Page to add your place of work. You'll be able to choose it from the drop-down menu. *If it doesn't appear when you type its name into the box, try using your username instead, this is the bit that comes after the Facebook URL www.facebook.com/_____*

Click

Another promotion opportunity is to add your Facebook Page URL and a link to your website to the 'Website' area under your contact information on your personal Facebook profile.

Make use of Public Posts

If you are the face of your company and are happy to share your personal updates with customers as a way to make them feel more connected with you and your business but you do not wish to add them all as friends you may wish to make use of public posts. These are the posts that are written on your personal profile that can be viewed by anybody, not just people on your friends list. You are able to decide which posts you wish to share with your friends, a specific group of friends, or with the public by clicking the privacy setting to the

Click

right of your post as you publish it. You can use this to target your updates that are relevant with different audiences by only sharing posts to that specific group of people and in line with this Facebook allows you to create custom lists of people who are connected with you. If for example, you have a piece of business news or something that is occurring within your industry that you feel only a select group of friends would be interested in you are able to share that update purely with that demographic.

To create a custom list from the home page, head to the 'Explore' section on the left hand side; click 'Friends Lists' and then 'Create List.' You are then able to create a List Name for example 'Potential Customers' and enter the names of the people you wish to add to this list into the 'Members' section.

Click

You will now be able to easily interact with the people inside of these lists and keep your content highly relevant to those on the list. Remember to connect with those on the list by commenting on their posts and liking the content they put out, allowing you to connect more deeply with your peers, building relationships which will eventually pay off as part of your overall marketing strategy.

Pinned Posts

Facebook allows you to pin a single post to the top of your Page's timeline.

These posts stay at the top of your Page and any new status updates will appear underneath the pinned post until it is unpinned, and then it will fall back to its original

Click

chronological position in the timeline. Pinning a post is one of the easiest – and most effective – ways to ensure that your best and most important post is the first thing visitors see when they visit your Page. You may want to consider pinning posts such as special announcements and promotions and changing these frequently.

Repurpose and Repost Content

People check their news feeds at different times of the day and only a small number of your followers will see your content first time you should get into the habit of repurposing and reposting your content. This will save you time in the long run too, seen as you won't have as much content to make if you reuse some of your existing posts. Do make an effort to change the posts slightly, a different link, or

Click

image, and changing up the text, as Facebook will consider your posts spam if you publish the same status over and over.

Embed Posts for Interaction outside of Facebook

Facebook gives the ability to embed posts on websites; this feature allows you to embed all public statuses, photos and videos so that your followers are able to interact directly with the embedded content without leaving your . site. You can use embedded posts to encourage interaction with your statuses in places away from Facebook, for example on a blog post or in an email. If the status update is public, anybody can then embed it from your Facebook Page or re-embed it from wherever else it appears – which could give your content a lot of exposure. Embedded posts include

Click

buttons for people to like, comment or share the post and also come with a button for people to like your page. To embed a post, go to the post that you wish to embed, click on the top right of the post and select embed, copy and paste the code that appears and add it to your own website.

Add Timeline Milestones

Facebook allows you to add Milestones in the history of your business (past and present) by scrolling through and marking dates on your timeline. You can Milestone the date your business first started trading, your 100th order, reaching a Milestone number of fans. You can use these to connect to your customers and provide them with a reason to remain further engaged with your page for example, thanking them for helping you reach a milestone and

Click

getting them to check back further down the line for a special offer.

Utilise Groups to build your business

Facebook groups are a great way to strengthen relationships with existing customers and also attract new ones. They work similarly whether you create your own or join one of the millions that already exist. In order to use groups as a marketing resource you should focus your time into groups relating to your chosen industry, your aim should be to position yourself as a person of authority in your industry, you should be active, give help and be genuine. Over time, your knowledge and influence will be recognised to pique interest, perhaps enough for them to consider your product or service.

Another opportunity to use groups on a local level would be to join local community groups

Click

that focus on selling in your particular niche. Most of us will be able to find a community group set up for their town or city The important thing about groups to remember is to use them appropriately. Take the time to learn who is using the groups and what they are interested in.

Thank your followers and newest fans: Create a post thanking your newest followers and top fans periodically. Doing this adds a personal touch to your businesses communication and makes your business stand out as one who cares about their audience. To encourage further engagement on your Page, launch a fan of the month initiative. By highlighting one of your most loyal fans in this way, you are indirectly encouraging others to engage with you more, so that they

Click

can be featured another time. You could add a small prize for the winner to add an incentive.

Go Live

A well-planned Facebook Live broadcast is a great way to share thoughtful, long-form content that engages viewers, ultimately playing to the algorithm. keep in mind that it isn't always about how many people watch, but rather how many engage. A thousand views with only 10 engagements won't make Facebook (or you) as happy as 100 people engaging, commenting, and hitting those reactions during the broadcasts. A high number of interactions makes it more likely Facebook will put your live video and replay in front of a wider audience. Showing your audience how to do something related to your industry not only demonstrates your expertise, but also makes your live

Click

streams and your page resources for further information about that topic.

In the Video section of your Facebook page, add your replay to a playlist. Playlists let you organize videos into groups based on common themes or topics. Then you can easily share them with viewers who are interested in the replays of your live stream or specific topics.

The wonderful thing about producing any video is that you now have one piece of content that you can repurpose for multiple marketing pieces:

Use sound bites for images, Instagram Stories, news feed clips, and more so you can keep sharing your live video content on social media.

Incorporate your video into your email marketing. Share your latest live stream with your email-marketing list

Click

Embed the video on your website/blog. Blog posts incorporating video attract 3 x as many links as posts without video.

Click

5. Utilising YouTube

Despite rising competition YouTube is the most popular, video-sharing site in the world and was one of the first social media sites that allowed you to post videos that they had made into an online format. Since its introduction in 2005, the video sharing/social media site has been a platform for businesses in every industry, of every size to market their products to future prospects and customers. YouTube predates even smartphones and has allowed people to make a name for themselves in the online world. YouTube differs from most other major social networks in that it is not a feed-based platform. Instead, content is presented to users after it is actively searched for which presents an abundance of opportunities for your business.

Click

Even though most people don't think of YouTube primarily as a search engine, that's exactly what most visitors do on the site. YouTube's not just the second most popular website; it's also the second most popular search engine – topped only by Google, it's parent company. This means that the platform presents a huge potential for reach for your business.

Video has consistently proven itself as one of the best-performing forms of content and as mentioned previously, in terms of engagement, and just because you're creating them for YouTube doesn't mean that you can't repurpose your videos. These videos would be great for your other social profiles, your email marketing campaigns, your website and landing pages, and any other platforms or channels you might be using.

Click

If you sell products, it's a great way to showcase and promote them and all of their uses and it's a great platform for expanding your reach and generating more leads.

Setting up Your Account

If you don't have a YouTube account already, you can set it up using a Google account, or even from your Gmail account. Choose a YouTube username that reflects your brand for your channel URL - don't make it too long or complicated.

Create an engaging profile and 'about' section, use this to market your products and services to your audience, linking up to all of your other relevant social media accounts and web links. In your description include keyword rich language; let your audience know what they will gain from joining your channel, why they

Click

should subscribe and how often you upload.
Associate your website with your YouTube by visiting your *channel* settings and going into the *advanced* menu. In this advanced section you should include your channel keywords and terms that your viewers will be searching.

Brand your YouTube Channel

Brand your YouTube channel incorporating your niche in the process. People love consistency and the more you are consistent with both your channel and all graphics throughout your channel, the more people will want to stay and be part of your little world on YouTube.

Branding is basically you telling your story and your "why" through your copy, images and artwork on your channel. Spending a few minutes (or hours) on your branding, no matter where you are at with your channel helps to

Click

realign your focus, niche and why. Please note, this doesn't have to happen before starting your channel or before you move onto the other steps. Branding is something that will develop over time. But, it is important to start thinking about these things at the beginning.

Upload a square, high-resolution profile photo that is recognisable at smaller resolutions. If you have chosen to link your Google+ account to your YouTube Channel your Google+ profile will have automatically become your YouTube profile photo, you can edit this via Google+. Optimize your banner for use on all devices and make sure it is a reflection of your business.

Perfect your YouTube thumbnail

Video thumbnails might be small, but they are often considered one of the most important

Click

things you can focus on (after making your video) to successfully promote your videos across other social media platforms. Consider your YouTube thumbnail your business card for the page. It will show up not only on your homepage, but when people search for a specific video, and when a video is shared. When designing your thumbnails, use consider the following, to ensure they're as effective as possible:

Use simple, clear text that describes what your video is all about.

Embed your logo in one of the bottom corners. Use complimentary colours or make them bright.

Be consistent with your brand. Stick with the same font type, colour scheme, and/or general layout so your videos are easily recognisable as *your* brand.

Click

Create a trailer for your Channel

YouTube gives you the option of selecting one video to highlight at the top of your YouTube home page below your channel banner. This is a great opportunity to showcase either your BEST video or to create a channel trailer demonstrating the value proposition of your channel and give a glimpse of your personality. On trailers a larger portion of the video description is shown directly opposite them, use this space to describe what your business and channel has to offer, and include relevant links and a call to action.

Create Playlists

From the controls area of your main Channel page, build playlists to feature your best and most viewed content. This also ensures that people view a series of videos in the order that

Click

they were intended to be played. Playlists lure viewers into watching more of your content and encourage multiple video views in one singular session. Group videos by topic in a playlist and name it something that demonstrates the value to the audience.

Create Intrigue

YouTube makes it easy for viewers to click away onto other peoples content. Create excitement and intrigue within the opening seconds to keep viewers watching your content.

Keep your introductions short. Long and boring introductions turn viewers off! Jump straight into the content of your video to keep viewers tuned in. Start all of your videos with a greeting, your name and business name and finish them with your business name and a call to action or tag-line, you could ask for

Click

subscribers to your channel, for them to give your video a like, or for them to take some direct action such as sharing the video or clicking a link.

Feature Calls to Actions

You can decide where in the video they would be best placed, but call to actions direct your viewers to making that next step and since you are putting content onto YouTube for a purpose within your business you should get into the practice of directing viewers to taking the next step. *Do you want them to visit your website, contact you for a quote, reply to a question in the comments, book in with you for a chat, subscribe for more great content, or click a link in the description?* – You need to tell them! Call to actions can be implemented in lots of different ways on YouTube, you can link directly from the video, inside the

Click

descriptions or in on-screen graphics such as an end card. You can create annotations to drive traffic from inside your videos. These work great to direct people to click through to your Call to Action.

Utilise Cards and End Screens

Cards are preformatted notifications that appear on desktop and mobile which you can set up to promote your brand and other videos on your channel. You can choose from a variety of card types like: merchandise, fundraising, video, playlist, website and more. Once they're set up, a small rectangular box, or teaser, will appear in the top right corner of the video to give your fans a preview of the message. If viewers tap or click the teaser, the card associated with the video appears along the right side of your video (or below the player on mobile in portrait mode).

Click

Cards work well when they are placed in conjunction with scripted calls to action or when they are relevant to your video content. For example, if you mention a specific video or a product, you could add a card at that exact moment. Cards are convenient because they give the viewer an option to click, and if they don't, it disappears from their view. At any point a user can click to see all cards that are applied to the video, which is handy if your viewer wants to continue watching the video but click through at another point.

You should use cards with the end experience for the viewer in mind, don't space them too far together otherwise you risk bombarding your viewer with too much information which won't be effective.

End Screens allow you to promote up to four elements. End Screens can be used to point

Click

viewers to other videos, playlists or channels on YouTube; to call for subscriptions to your channel and to promote your website and/or products. End screens and cards are most successful when they give your viewers something relevant to watch or do. When you add a card or end screen, ensure it points or gives context to the thing that your viewer may want to do next.

Both end screens and cards let you:

Feature other relevant videos on your channel or another video you like on YouTube. You can select a video you want to feature manually, or, *with end screens*, YouTube can do this for you by selecting either the latest upload or the best option for your viewer.

Direct viewers to more information like content on your website, your products or crowd

Click

funding campaign, or other websites important to your channel.

Highlight collaborators by adding channel cards.

Ask questions or get feedback for market research purposes using poll cards.

End screens only appear in the last 20 seconds of your videos, but you can use cards throughout.

Make the most of cards by setting them up to appear at a relevant time in your video. For example, you could promote something to watch next or another channel you think your viewers might like to watch, but try to make sure that you're not asking them to leave at the most exciting part of your video! Cards work best if they appear later in your video when your viewers are looking for somewhere to go

Click

next. You can try these tips for animation at the perfect moment:

Set video cards to animate in the last 20% of your video, just before you are wrapping up, so that viewers see them before they move on to the next video. Note: Cards won't animate if used at the same time as an end screen.

Set product link cards to appear when your products appear in the video.

If you are using multiple cards, space them out for a good end viewer experience.

Post Videos Regularly and Consistently

To stay in the forefront of viewers' minds, many content creators have found that setting

Click

a routine publishing schedule helps viewers to know when to expect their next release – it's like anticipating the next episode of your favourite show. In order to build traction and maintain your presence aim to publish at set intervals *(such as weekly)* and on certain days *(for example every Tuesday)*

You are able to batch record your content and then upload those videos, schedule the date, time and time zone for their publication. Depending on the purpose of your channel and your marketing goals you may decide to keep flexible enough to respond to search trends, breaking news or viral video trends.

Subscribers to your channel are able to find your new uploads in their Subscriptions feed, and can opt-in to mobile or email notifications based on their interests. Let your viewers know when you plan to release new videos.

Click

You can let them know inside your videos, video descriptions, channel trailer and in the about section, for example.

Find other ways to stay active on your channel If you don't have time to produce new videos constantly, you can still interact with your fans in other ways. When reading comments, consider joining in the conversation so that your viewers feel a part of your brand and know you're listening. You can do this by:

Interacting with comments: try posting comments on your own videos, as well as replying to comments from others. You can pin your favourite comment to the top of the feed. The YouTube Studio app allows you to reply to comments on the go.

Setting aside time for your channel activity: If you upload videos weekly, you may decide to schedule a certain day or time of day for fan

Click

interactions, such as adding hearts to your favourite comments.

Maximising your shoots: as mentioned earlier in the book consider block shooting more than one video during your production days so that you have some queued up and scheduled for release.

Shooting extra footage: then repurposing it later in short-format videos. You can use this content for things like bloopers, behind-the-scenes, recaps, snippets, trailers and more. You are able to adjust your Community settings if you want to hold and review new comments before they're posted. You can select users whose comments will be automatically approved.

Cross Post

Click

YouTube is easily integrated into other social media platforms, making it easy to share content you have already recorded whilst also strengthening relationships and attracting new audiences on those social media platforms too. Cross posting also drives more traffic to back to your channel.

Don't Skip the SEO

Google owns YouTube; this means that YouTube is essentially a search engine of its own, which means that SEO (search engine optimization) is key to making sure your videos are reaching new audiences.

You'll want to make sure your content is being found by the types of people who are searching for it, by including target keywords in your video titles and description. The same goes for your channel description.

Click

This not only means your lists, metadata, description, and the videos themselves, but also your transcripts, closed captions, and subtitles. It is important to remember that your content is searchable both inside and out of YouTube. So, by making sure your videos are optimised, you'll also give potential customers the chance to stumble upon your content when searching for other things on Google.

When coming up with a title for your videos, think about what your audience is likely to search for and reflect that in the words you use. Your video should be *keyword rich* and match the *content* that your video contains. Only the first 45 characters of the video title are displayed in the YouTube search results on a mobile device, so make sure you use primary keywords and phrases first.

Click

Add a colon after your initial keywords and then rephrase your title: For example a video on saving money on advertising could be "Save Money Easily on Marketing: The Simple money saving business plan." This will capture those people who are searching for videos using two similar (but different) phrases.

Use Keywords in your video content:

YouTube can understand what you say in your videos. And when YouTube hears you say your target keyword in your video, it helps them understand that your video is about that keyword and it ranks your content higher. Get into the habit of mentioning your main keyword twice when recording your videos. You can also upload a transcript of your video to make sure that YouTube is picking up on your keywords correctly.

Click

Tag your videos: Tags are descriptive keywords that help people to find your content, the more relevant your tags the more discoverable your video will be.

Write effective video descriptions: The first few sentences of your descriptions will appear in YouTube search results, and the same lines will appear below your content on the video's individual page followed by a "see more" link that must be clicked to read the rest. As discussed already it's good practice to include keyword rich descriptions in the first one or two sentences. For those who click through to read your description in full, consider adding the following information to all of your video descriptions:

A description of your channel and a link to your channel page

Click

A call to action asking viewers to subscribe with a link to click

Links to more episodes or your playlists

Information about your channel upload video schedules for example "New video uploads every Wednesday."

Links to your social media accounts with an enticing call to action to follow you

When adding links in your video descriptions make sure you use the full URL including the 'http://' prefix. Otherwise YouTube will not automatically hyperlink it and then it won't be clickable.

Ask for subscribers

Ask for subscribers to your channel at the end of every video.

Click

If someone has watched your content all the way to the end of your video, they are primed to hit that subscribe button, sometimes all they need is a little nudge, asking them to subscribe as a call to action is that nudge.

Embed a YouTube widget onto your blog or website

A YouTube subscribe widget is a box that you can embed onto your website to encourage people to subscribe to your channel, or click through to check it out. It acts as a permanent advertisement that you have a channel and you can also embed playlists to always display your most popular content furthering increasing it's impact.

Click

Popular Video Marketing Strategies

Record product demos and reviews: rather than telling people what your product or service can do, why not show them?

Convert podcasts into YouTube videos: If you already have a podcast for your business, you can turn them into videos and upload them to YouTube to expand your reach. YouTube doesn't allow you to upload audio alone, so consider recording the podcast in video format or creating some topical slides with relevant information for viewers.

Be topical with news: Show your expertise in your field by reacting and discussing breaking news and information.

Creating a video series: If you can split your topic into a video series doing so will keep your viewers engaged over a number of days

Click

or weeks. Give your viewers the tools they need to subscribe and find the other videos in the series. Like a Netflix series viewers can either tune in as your content is released or sit and binge the whole series.

Click

6. Capturing Followers on Instagram

Instagram is a powerful marketing tool for those who are patient and persistent enough to learn how to use it's features to connect with their audience. Since it's launch in October 2010 hundreds of millions of people use Instagram as a way to transform and share everyday photographs and videos with the use of filters and frames into memories that are then shared with the world.

With the right Instagram strategy marketers are able to tap into this, increasing brand loyalty and then driving sales as a result. Instagram is quite often referred to as "The Worlds most powerful Selling Tool" due to the level of passion that many of its users show.

Click

They are young; they are engaged with social media and many of them are online shoppers. Instagram users tend to be more engaged than the average social media user with users producing higher interaction and engagement rates compared to both Facebook and Twitter.

This chapter will focus on Instagram, however many of the tips and strategies shared can apply to other methods of photo sharing or mini-video sharing on social media.

Understanding Instagram

Top performing marketers on Instagram all have one thing in common; they understand what makes Instagram unique from other social media platforms.

Click

Whilst there will always be the potential for the app to develop over time, at it's core the users who are the most successful post thought-out quality content rather than impulsive and quick content. The users with the most impressive followings use their time to carefully construct photo moments so that when they do share it to their Instagram feed, it's speaks exactly to their target audience and so it then gets complimented on with comments, likes and new followers.

Since it's foundation the very culture and concept at Instagram has been to 'make everyday moments beautiful' and since cameras and smart phones improved so have their users desire to share those photos. For those responsible for marketing in their business, this has meant sharing how your company or business sees the world, sharing

Click

images that pushes deeper understandings of your products, services and values and offering a view into the lifestyle that your product or service makes possible, through your own eyes, but also through the eyes of the customers that use them.

As mentioned earlier in the book to create a successful Instagram marketing strategy you will need to know what you wish to accomplish with your posts and who you wish to reach. You can narrow your focus by answering the following questions:

How would you describe your business to a friend?
What makes your business unique?
Who are your customers?

Click

What do you need them to know about your services or products?

What is the goal of your account?

When planning your content and strategy whether that's for stories, your feed, IGTV or for your bio you should be certain on your brands core message and what you want to make your audience think and what you want them to feel when they see your content. We'll touch on this later in this chapter.

Instagram is a place that people go to discover and become inspired by the photo's they see. Posting just any image on Instagram will not lead to the results you'll want as a marketer, it definitely pays in the long term to be more selective with the content you are sharing.

Click

One of the easiest ways to understand what Instagram really wants from the content on its platform is to look at their guidelines for Instagram ads:

Photographs should capture 'moment's not products. In other words, ads should not just be an image of your product but something more creative.

Brands cannot feature their logo in an overly dominant way other than in a natural way that could be part of the scene.

Images used as advertisements on Instagram must be in keeping with your brand.

No heavy use of image filters as a way to mask the reality of the image.

No text overlays are allowed.

As you build your own Instagram strategy, keep these guidelines in mind. As with all

Click

strategies they won't work in every situation, all of the time but they are a good starting foundation to building content that your clients are going to want to get excited about on Instagram.

Your Instagram images should be creative enough to showcase your brand's personality but well crafted enough to appeal to your audience. Find ways to incorporate your logo, icon or a colour into your style to increase familiarity with your posts. You can also take a series of images that tell a story about your brand and share them across a period of time and tell a story.

With some practice, anyone can create compelling images.

Some things to consider when creating your images:

Click

Create a single focal point: Avoid making your images too busy. Crop your photo to direct people's attention to the most important part of the image. One focal point of the picture should include the brand logo or a brand element that is easily recognisable to your audience.

Use contrasting colors: Use props or backgrounds to draw attention to your subject. Pair colors that complement each other and stand out in people's feeds.

Experiment with unconventional angles and perspectives: Arrange any objects in an intriguing way to attract attention. You could photograph products from above, choose a lower angle, get up close to the subject or place it in a corner of the frame.

Think about your lighting: Use high resolution and clear images. Pictures with bad

Click

lighting, flaws or that are highly pixelated won't perform as well and doesn't give out a professional message about your brand.

Framing: Straighten out images to make sure they look clean. Consider using symmetry, the rule of thirds or other photograph composition basics when crafting images for Instagram.

Think in squares: Before Instagram came into our lives, most of our pictures were either landscape or portrait and followed a set of rules photographers swore by. But some of these rules don't necessarily apply to square-shaped photos. Before you press the shutter on your image take a moment to consider how your image will look as a square. You don't want to crop out a critical element of your content. You are now able to publish photographs and video content in landscape or portrait mode too.

Click

Zoom in on details: When marketing your services and products you cannot get away from the fact that most of your users will be viewing your content from a mobile device. This offers a relatively small area of space to work with. You may wish to zoom or focus on a particular detail of the product or service you are photographing in order to convey your message more effectively.

Think about the composition: Look at the scene with your naked eye, rather than through the lens this is because your brain naturally picks out subjects of interest. Choose your subject, isolate it from the background clutter and make it the centre of attention in the frame before you press the click.

Make sure your camera lens is clean: This may sound obvious but the reason the photographs you take are blurry and out of

Click

focus could be as simple as a dirty camera lens. Phones get quite dirty; improving your photography skills could start with something as simple as a quick wipe of the lens.

Use your headphones cable for perfect focus every time: When taking a picture using your phone it's easy to jolt the screen losing the framing and focus. To avoid this, you can use your headphones, plug them in and touch the 'volume up' button to take a photograph whilst in the camera app.

The best marketers on Instagram are extremely choosey about the images they share on their accounts. Quality definitely beats quantity on this platform. Take your time to create a collection of photographs that will stand out when viewed individually in algorithm collected news feeds but also as your gallery is viewed as a whole from your profile.

Click

Optimising your account for success

Your Instagram bio is like a modern day business card, portfolio and a website home page all wrapped up into one. First impressions count and Instagram gives users just 150 characters to give your visitors a reason to follow you.

A good Instagram bio explains what your business is and what you do in just a couple of sentences.

Whilst you might only get 150 characters to play around with in your bio, that doesn't mean it can't get you more followers.

And not just *any* followers, with a fine-tuned bio, you can target your ideal audience so any new visitors will be able to quickly understand what you and your business are all about. And if they like what they see, they're more likely to tap the follow button!

Click

It's also a good idea to focus your Instagram bio copy on how you help or inspire your ideal followers; by writing an Instagram bio that speaks directly to your target audience, you'll attract more quality followers who are aligned with your brand and more likely to become customers.

Your Instagram bio is the perfect place to make your brand or business stand out for a particular skill, profession, hobby, or interest — it's a place to add a little bit of personality alongside your business pitch.

Use the Name Field to Share Top Keywords

The name field in your Instagram bio is totally separate to the username and handle.

Choosing to just use your Instagram handle - *the part of URL that takes followers directly to your feed* as your name field is a lost

Click

marketing opportunity as name fields are fully searchable in Instagram.

Including relevant keywords is a much better strategy for your brand if you want to be discovered and get more followers. Think about the keywords that your followers are searching for on Instagram whether that's maybe your business niche or the products you sell. Once you find the right keywords, put them into your name field to ensure that you rank when those words are searched for.

Add a Call-To-Action for the Link in Your

Instagram Bio

Instagram only gives you one link on your profile; it's a good idea to use that last line of text to give visitors a reason to click your link.

Click

If you're offering a new promo, resource, or limited time offer, make sure to let your profile visitors know. If it aligns with your brand, use a mixture of text and emojis to drive attention to the link. You only have 150 characters, so don't be afraid to use emojis to save space and add some personality to your profile. Many top Instagram accounts are now deliberately choosing to include a link to their blog rather than directly to a product or shop, showing that they have a longer term goal of building a brand image and relationship rather than focusing on a quick sale. The link in bio and bio copy can be changed enabling you to focus on sharing different links for your business at the right time for your ideal client.

Include multiple links in bio

Instagram only allows you to include one link in your bio to drive traffic to an external site

Click

outside of the platform. However you are able to use external tools to include multiple links in order to drive traffic. These tools create clickable links or landing pages easily redirecting your visitors to specific products, pages, shops or services you mention in your content.

Optimise your profile photo

The profile photo is as important as your bio in making that first impression. All profile photos should be a perfect square at 110 x 110 pixels. You can check that your Instagram profile picture looks on brand in a circle in the "Edit Profile" section from your profile.

You'll see a preview of a perfect circle and what your profile picture will look like once cropped - just make sure the focus of your Instagram profile picture is within the circular

Click

frame - Everything that's in the grey area will be cropped out

You may want to consider using your brand logo as your profile picture. This can help with your brand recognition and will make sure that everyone who lands on your Instagram account is quickly introduced to your logo and banding. If you offer a service you may wish to use a headshot as your Instagram profile picture so that your followers get a quick and effective introduction to you from the second they land on your account.

Your Instagram profile picture should fit with your overall Instagram theme and aesthetic. Edited your profile photo in the same way as your other images and if you are sticking to a specific colour palette for your brand, try to include this in your profile picture too.

Click

If you are using a headshot, you can do this by wearing a top in your brand colours or by editing your image to include a ring of colour or banner within your image.

Instagram Marketing Strategy

Post consistently: There is no magic formula as the right time to post on Instagram but, there certainly is a wrong time to post. Uncover when your followers are most active by using the Insights feature of your Instagram Business or Creator account. This helps you identify when your followers are most active and allows you to schedule accordingly, ensuring your posts continue to appear at the top of their feeds.

Tell Stories: Capture attention through images, video, and text that tell stories rather than just content that sells. Offer micro-stories via your captions, videos, Instagram stories

Click

and profile. When people feel an emotional connection to your content, they are much more likely to buy into it and share it with their peers.

One way to insert elements of storytelling into your Instagram strategy is by sharing user-generated content that resonates with your brand. Another way is to focus on telling a story with your captions. Done right, wordy captions also stop scrollers in their feeds and increase the time they spend looking at your post. Provide the content that aligns with what your audience cares about or help them with their problems. Do it well by embracing different content formats, such as stories, IGTV, videos, photos, and captions.

Choose the right hashtags: Using hashtags in your captions or comments will place your

Click

content with other content using the same hashtag. They also turn into clickable links so you can see those photo sets. Users seek out content on Instagram using hashtags and so using the right hashtags can help your target audience find your products and services when they search for relevant keywords and phrases.

Make it easy for users to find your content by ensuring that the hashtags you use accurately describe your content. Use a mix of trending and industry-specific hashtags to find the best hashtag to connect with your targeted followers. Utilise descriptive and specific hashtags to give your content a much better chance of being found.

Create a branded hashtag: A branded hashtag is great way to build a culture around

Click

your brand. The best starting point is a general brand hashtag. It should be short, memorable and include your brand name in some form. Having a branded hashtag makes your content more discoverable; drive traffic to your profile and creating a stronger community around your brand. It will also help you organize your content, making it easily findable and trackable.

Place the hashtag in your bio so that it is easy to find.

Increase your reach with Geotags: Geotags are often overlooked but can give you a little edge when trying to reach more people. By adding a location tag to your photo, you are essentially pinning your location to that post. Anytime a user clicks on that geotag on another photo your post will also be found in

Click

that content. To geotag your content tap add location from your post feed and choose from the list or type a location of your choice.

If you are aiming to target users within a particular location you can use this feature to engage with and be inspired by top performing content in that area. For example creating a piece of content around a landmark or stunning piece of scenery and linking it to your service or product or connecting with users in that location.

Embed your Instagram photos and videos: When viewing a piece of content on Instagram from a desktop browser, you are able to copy and paste an embed code over to your website or blog. The image will also feature an embedded Instagram logo which then when

Click

clicked will take viewers to your Instagram profile where they can discover more of your content.

Use Instagram Shopping Tags: Instagram Shopping gives businesses a storefront for users to explore their best products. With Instagram Shopping, you can share featured products through organic posts and Stories, or have people discover products in Search & Explore. When someone taps a product tag they'll be taken to a product description page where they will see:

An image of the product

A description of the product and the price

How much the product costs

A link that takes them directly to purchase the product

Click

By enabling Shopping posts, shoppers are free to move from inspiration to decision quickly and without distraction.

Gain insight of your insights: Understanding the insights of your account over time enables you to develop a content strategy that works. It's much more than just finding out which post, video or story performed the best! In case you needed another reason to switch over to a business profile insights are only available on business accounts. Delving into your analytics allows you to understand what your audience responds so then you are able to drive more traffic and sales. For example Let's say your insights showed that more of a younger audience were viewing and appreciating your content, you may wish to post more frequently

Click

as younger demographics tend to use Instagram in short bursts throughout the day. You may also use pop culture references, incorporate gifs and memes into your content. If you have a global audience, in non-English speaking countries you may want to adjust your content to have less copy for a deeper better understanding.

Video on Instagram

As mentioned in other chapters, video marketing is a highly effective strategy and it's no different for Instagram. When Instagram launched the ability to load video content 5 million were published within the first 24 hours and with video views up year on year it's fairly clear to see that the marketing potential of incorporating video into your overall strategy is huge. However with videos being able to be shared in a variety of ways on Instagram it's

Click

easy to become overwhelmed as to what kind of strategy to adopt for your particular business and ideal client.

Videos shared in your feed can be up to 60 seconds long but you are able to upload videos that are longer or shorter by using stories, live video or IGTV.

Insta-Feed video: If you want to upload a video onto your Instagram feed and have it show up like a normal photo on your Instagram profile, you should choose a video to upload a video that is less than 60 seconds. You are able to upload videos that are longer but as videos included in your feed are only a minute long, choose a portion of the video that you would like to post.

Instagram Stories: videos shared on Instagram stories can only be 15 seconds long, making them perfect to share smaller

Click

messages with your audience and not have them show up on your actual feed. Videos longer than 15 seconds will be automatically split into separate segments and uploaded into separate videos.

Livestream: these can be viewed for up to a maximum of 60 minutes. When you hit live on Instagram your video will automatically record and save so you are able to reshare the video with your followers direct to your feed or you may wish to disable the rewatch feature.

IGTV: Most marketers on Instagram will have between 15 seconds and 10 minutes to share. Those with larger followings or verified accounts are able to share up to an hour of video using this feature.

Reels: Currently you are able to upload videos up to 30 seconds using Reels. A fairly new feature to most accounts, reels seems to focus

Click

on sharing more entertaining bite-size pieces of content.

In order to decide what kind of video marketing is right for your business it's important to clearly understand your brand image and the story you want to tell to your followers and ensure that the content matches the feel and overall look of your brand. Consistency as always is key! As mentioned previously, given the effort required producing video, you shouldn't create it "just because." Instead, think about the goals behind your video content.

For example are you looking to drive more traffic to your website or store? Create brand awareness? Increase followers? Increase views?

Marketers don't need expensive equipment or huge budgets to create video on Instagram,

Click

simplicity again works best, getting laser focused on the message you are delivering and sharing that in as concise a way as possible.

 Some ideas of the types of video you may wish to create for your audience include:

Product or service videos: easily show the bonuses of using your product or services offer an explainer video such as a 'how to' or create a video of the product in action. Incorporate sneak previews of any new releases you have coming allowing your audience to feel a part of the journey and have them wanting to come back for more before your product is even available.

Take your followers behind the scenes: Simplicity is key and there's nothing simple than a quick shot of the behind the scenes of

Click

your day using stories. This enables customers to feel more connected to your business or brand and incorporating story features such as stickers, time stamps and gifs makes your content feel more authentic. Showcasing behind the scenes content is a great way to build more personal relationships with your followers and by introduction your followers to the team and giving them exclusive content you are able to showcase your brand values in a more authentic way.

Answer a Q and A session: *Sharing simple question and answer short videos requires no equipment, other than your smartphone and additionally allows you to directly interact with your audience. You could have viewers ask questions in a live stream or source them in advance using the questions feature on*

Click

stories. You can do this to build interest before launch or incorporate it into your overall *getting to know you* strategy.

Click

7. Quick Tips for Continued Success

Social Media is an ever changing and growing sector. In this book we have focused on 3 of the main social media channels that marketers can use to stay ahead of the game and focus on social media. Going forward there will definitely be changes coming. The very nature of this book means that some of the tips relating to the platforms we have looked into in more detail may become outdated in the future. However, the strategies inside of this book will help you come up with a bullet proof social media plan to create and market to your tribe on whichever platform you choose

Click

despite the changes to individual features and ever new channels.

Within this final chapter we'll go over some of the tips we have covered in order to help with your continued success on the platforms you choose.

Define your goals and objectives

If you don't know what you want, how are you supposed to achieve it? Not to mention, you can't measure, change or evolve your strategies over time if you don't have strong goals to begin with.

Your social media goals should align with your overall marketing efforts.

Research your audience

Connecting and engaging with your audience is crucial in today's marketing if you want to create a profit.

Click

But, in order to do that, you need to understand your audience – inside and out. You should be able to pinpoint their needs, wants, and desires clearly and do this often as your business services and product progresses

Craft your content carefully

Take the time to learn about the platforms you are investing your time in and create content that is appropriate for the platform and the demographics that use it. Part of crafting your content will involve the words that you use. Direct your captions to your audience directly.

Avoid overly salesy marketing techniques

This kind of marketing got outdated a long time ago and for good reason. Customers want to get to know your business and make a

Click

connection to your message and values. Once your customers trust you, they'll buy from you.

Promotion is key to your entire strategy

You could create the most mind-blowing, quality content on the Internet – but if nobody ever sees it, you're not going to see results. That's where promotion comes in.

Cross promote your accounts between your other social profiles

Collaborate with influencers in your industry

Run a social media contest that encourages participants to follow you

Leverage other platforms you have access to (for example, after someone subscribes to your email list, invite them to follow you on social media.)

Take a SEO-driven approach to the content you publish on social networks (for example;

Click

use relevant hashtags on Instagram and use popular keywords in titles/descriptions for YouTube.)

Social media marketing is by no means a passive form of advertising. But the benefits are difficult to ignore.

Use the social media marketing tips to fine-tune your strategy until you've created a winning strategy and always keep in the forefront of your mind that social networks are made for conversing with others and not just for selling and you'll be half-way there in building a tribe around your product or service on social media.

Click

Printed in Great Britain
by Amazon